CW00392199

High Protein Bodybuilding

VEGETARIAN

COOKBOOK

**Delicious Plant-Based Meals to Help You Reach Your
Protein Goals**

Theresa Lynch

Copyright © [2023] [Theresa Lynch]

All rights reserved. This book or any portion thereof may not be reproduced or used in any manner whatsoever without the express written permission of the author except for the use of brief quotations in a book review. This book is a work of non-fiction and is for informational purposes only. It is not intended to provide medical advice or to be used in any way to diagnose, treat, or cure any medical condition. The author and publisher shall not be liable for any errors or omissions in this book.

Copyright Theresa Lynch, 2022

Table of contents

Introduction

Vegetarian Meal Prep Basics

    High Protein Creamy Spinach Mushroom Pasta Bake

    Vegan Stuffed Butternut Squash with Lentil Apple Filling

    Vegetarian Stuffed Peppers

    Buffalo Tempeh Salad

    Homemade ricotta gnocchi

    Overnight Breakfast Casserole With Bacon And Sweet Potatoes

    Kidney Bean Curry (Jamaican-Style)

    Chickpea Noodle Soup

    High Protein Greek Yogurt Pasta Sauce

    Halloumi Burrito Bowl With Roasted Potatoes

    Savory Oatmeal

    Spicy Black Bean Burger

    Mapo Tofu

    Rican Rice and Beans

    Brown Rice Veggie Bowl With Crispy Tofu

    Vegetable Tofu Scramble

    Black-Eyed Pea Fritters

    Oven Roasted Broccoli

    Aubergine and Lentil Vegetarian Moussaka

    Tofu Bolognese

    Vegan Stuffed Peppers

Lentil Tacos

Black Bean Burrito Bowl

Vegetarian Toad in the Hole

Baked Feta with Veggies

Beetroot Pasta

Heavenly Halloumi Salad

Cheese and Spinach Pie

Flawless Feta and Spinach Pancakes

Vegan Chickpea Winter Salad

Smoked Tofu & Hummus Buddha Bowl

Healthy Egg Salad

Homemade Ramen in a Jar

Vegetarian Banh Mi

Spinach Tomato Quesadillas

Vegetarian Greek Pitas

Chickpea Salad Sandwich

Vegetarian Wedge Salad

Lentil Tabbouleh

Best High-protein Tangy Tempeh Salad

Chickpea Spinach Salad

Black Bean Lime Dip

Carrot and Red Lentil Soup

Lentil Salad

Blueberry Banana Protein Smoothie

Perfect Scrambled Eggs with Cheese

Couscous Kaiserschmarrn

Beans and Eggs

10-Minute Vegan Tempeh Sandwich

Fresh & Minty Pineapple and Spinach Smoothie

Bread Pudding

Spinach and Chickpea Bake

German Bauernfrühstuck

Creamy Cashew Milkshake

High Protein Yogurt Breakfast with Raspberry Compote

Smoked Tofu Breakfast Egg

Volume Conversions

Introduction

Welcome!

This comprehensive guide is designed to help you make delicious, nutritious, and convenient vegetarian high protein meals without having to sacrifice time or effort.

Whether you're a novice cook or a seasoned chef, this cookbook is perfect for anyone looking to create healthy, satisfying meals without breaking the bank. Inside, you'll find easy-to-follow recipes that can be cooked in advance and stored for later use. With a variety of ingredients and spices, you'll be able to craft tasty dishes that will leave you feeling full and satisfied.

Meal prepping is a great way to save time and money, as well as to ensure that you're getting a balanced diet. This cookbook is full of recipes that will make meal prepping a breeze. We'll show you how to make delicious high protein vegetarian dishes that are packed with essential nutrients and flavors.

In addition to providing easy-to-follow recipes, this cookbook also offers helpful tips and tricks for maximizing your meal prepping experience. We'll show you how to save time and money while making sure that you're getting all of the nutrition you need. From stocking your pantry with the right ingredients to using kitchen gadgets and shortcuts, we'll give you the tools you need to make meal prepping easier and more efficient.

So, let's get started! With this cookbook, you'll be able to create healthy, delicious vegetarian meals without having to spend hours in the kitchen. Whether you're looking for a quick lunch, a hearty dinner, or a tasty snack, you'll find the perfect recipe for it here. Get ready to embark on a journey of deliciousness!

Vegetarian Meal Prep Basics

High-protein vegetarian meal prep basics provide an important source of nutrition for those who want to maintain a healthy and balanced diet while still avoiding animal products. Eating a diet rich in plant-based proteins can help you reach your health goals while still enjoying delicious and nutritious meals.

When it comes to meal prepping as a vegetarian, it's important to make sure you are getting enough protein. Protein is essential for building and maintaining muscle, and it plays an important role in many of our body's functions. With vegetarian meal prepping, it's important to include high-protein foods that are also packed with other essential nutrients.

Here are some of the basics you should include in your vegetarian meal prep:

Legumes: Legumes are an excellent source of plant-based protein and fiber. They are also packed with vitamins and minerals, making them a great addition to any meal. Some of the most popular legumes include lentils, beans, peas, and chickpeas. These can be used in a variety of dishes, from salads and soups to veggie burgers and tacos.

Nuts and seeds: Nuts and seeds provide a great source of plant-based protein, as well as healthy fats and fiber. Almonds, walnuts, cashews, and sunflower seeds are some of the most popular options. They can be eaten plain, added to salads and other dishes, or made into nut butters.

Whole grains: Whole grains are a great source of complex carbohydrates and fiber. They also provide a variety of vitamins and minerals. Quinoa, oatmeal, and brown rice are some of the most popular options. These can be used in salads, stir-fries, and more.

Vegetables: Vegetables are an essential part of any healthy diet. They are packed with vitamins and minerals and are low in calories. Some of the most nutrient-dense vegetables include spinach, kale, broccoli, Brussels sprouts, and cauliflower. These can be added to salads, soups, stir-fries, and more.

Soy products: Soy products are an excellent source of plant-based protein. Tofu, tempeh, and edamame are some of the most popular options. These can be used in a variety of dishes, from stir-fries and salads to veggie burgers and tacos.

These are just a few of the basics you should include in your vegetarian meal prep. There are also other plant-based proteins, such as seitan and textured vegetable protein, that can be used in a variety of dishes. With the right combination of ingredients, you can create delicious and nutritious meals that will help you reach your health goals.

High Protein Creamy Spinach Mushroom Pasta Bake

Servings : 6

17 grams Protein

50 grams Carb

17 grams Fat

412 Cal Per Serving

Est. Prep Time: 5 mins

Est. Cook Time: 25 mins

Est. Total Time: 30 mins

Ingredients

- 12 oz pasta uncooked
- 2 tablespoons unsalted butter
- 1 small onion diced
- 1 pound mushrooms of choice thinly sliced
- 2 cloves garlic minced
- 3 cups baby spinach
- 1 teaspoon italian seasoning
- 1/2 tsp salt

- 1/4 tsp pepper
- 1 tablespoon all-purpose flour
- 1/2 cup vegetable broth or water
- 1 cup light cream or half and half
- 1/4 cup freshly grated Parmesan
- 1 cup mozzarella cheese
- 2 tablespoons chopped fresh parsley leaves

Instructions

- Heat the oven to 375F. Cook pasta as directed on the package in a big pot of boiling, salted water. Drain well. Place aside.
- In a large skillet over medium heat, melt the butter. Cook the onion and mushrooms for two to three minutes, or until the mushrooms are cooked. Italian seasoning, garlic, spinach, salt, and

pepper should all be added. one more minute of cooking.

- For approximately a minute, whisk in the flour until just just browned. Vegetable broth and cream should be added gradually while whisking continuously throughout the first one to two minutes of cooking. Just before turning off the heat, stir in the parmesan.

- Put the cooked spaghetti in a 13 x 9-inch baking dish. Add spinach, mushroom, and cream sauce on top. Add mozzarella cheese drizzle. Bake till bubbling for 18 to 20 minutes.

Vegan Stuffed Butternut Squash with Lentil Apple Filling

Servings : 4

12 grams Protein

48 grams Carb

9 grams Fat

298 Cal Per Serving

Est. Prep Time: 10 mins

Est. Cook Time: 50 mins

Est. Total Time: 60 mins

Ingredients

- 1 large Butternut Squash or two small butternut squashes
- 2 tsp oil
- 1/4 tsp salt
- generous dash of black pepper

For the Filling:

- 1 tsp oil
- 1/4 tsp fennel seeds preferably crushed

- 1/4 tsp dried sage or 1 tbsp chopped fresh sage
- 1/2 tsp dried thyme
- 1/4 tsp dried rosemary
- 1/4 cup (40 g) of finely chopped red onion
- 2 cloves garlic finely chopped
- 15 oz can of lentils drained, or 1.5 cups cooked lentils
- 1/2 tsp salt
- 1/4 tsp onion powder
- 1/8 tsp black pepper
- 1/2 of an apple chopped small
- 1/4 cup (27.25 g) chopped pecans

Instructions

- Butternut squash should be cut in half. After removing the seed box, spritz, brush, and season with salt and pepper.

- Bake for 45 to 50 minutes, or until the center is fully done, at 400 degrees F (205 C).
- Make your lentil stuffing in the interim. Fennel seeds, sage, thyme, and rosemary should be added to a skillet that has been heated over medium heat along with the oil.
- Once combined, add the onion and garlic and heat until the onion turns golden.
- Add the lentils, salt, onion powder, and black pepper, and stir to combine. Next, add the apples and pecans, stir to combine, and cook for an additional two to three minutes, or until the mixture is thoroughly heated. Taste, then modify flavor.
- Butternut squash should be taken out of the oven.

- Butternut squash should be cut in half. After removing the seed box, spritz, brush, and season with salt and pepper.
- Bake for 45 to 50 minutes, or until the center is fully done, at 400 degrees F (205 C).
- Make your lentil stuffing in the interim. Fennel seeds, sage, thyme, and rosemary should be added to a skillet that has been heated over medium heat along with the oil.
- Once combined, add the onion and garlic and heat until the onion turns golden.
- Add the lentils, salt, onion powder, and black pepper, and stir to combine. Next, add the apples and pecans, stir to combine, and cook for an additional two to three minutes, or until the mixture is thoroughly heated. Taste, then modify flavor.

- Butternut squash should be taken out of the oven.

Vegetarian Stuffed Peppers

Servings : 4

16.5 grams Protein

52.3 grams Carb

18.4 grams Fat

430 Cal Per Serving

Est. Prep Time: 20 mins

Est. Cook Time: 60 mins

Est. Total Time: 80 mins

Ingredients

- 4 large red bell peppers, halved from stem to base, seeds and membranes removed
- 1 tablespoon extra virgin olive oil, as needed
- Fine salt and freshly ground black pepper, for sprinkling
- ½ cup long-grain brown rice (or 1 ½ cups cooked rice)
- 2 tablespoons extra virgin olive oil

- 1 large yellow onion, chopped
- ½ teaspoon fine salt, to taste
- 1 pint (2 cups) cherry tomatoes, halved or quartered if large
- ½ cup chopped fresh cilantro, plus more for garnish
- 4 cloves garlic, pressed or minced
- 1 ½ teaspoons chili powder
- 1 teaspoon ground cumin
- 1 can (1 ½ cups) pinto beans, rinsed and drained
- Freshly ground black pepper, to taste
- 1 tablespoon lime juice
- 4 ounces (about 1 cup) grated part-skim mozzarella or cheddar

Instructions

- Preheat the oven to 425 degrees Fahrenheit before roasting the peppers. Put the peppers that have been cut in half in a sizable 9 by 13-inch baking dish or on a parchment-lined baking sheet with a rim. Add salt and pepper to the peppers and drizzle 1 tablespoon of olive oil over them. The peppers should be arranged with the sliced sides facing up after you use your hands to thoroughly rub the oil into both of them. Bake the peppers for 20 to 25 minutes, or until they are slightly blistered around the edges and punctured easily with a fork. Place aside. Keep the oven on so that the peppers can bake.

- Cook the rice in the interim by heating a sizable pot of water to a boil. In a colander with fine mesh, rinse the rice until the water is clear. The rice should be added to the boiling water and boiled for 30 minutes while being covered (reduce the heat as necessary to prevent overflow). Return the rice to the pot after draining the remaining cooking liquid. Place aside.

- To make the filling, heat 2 tablespoons of olive oil in a large skillet over medium heat until it shimmers. 12 teaspoon of salt and the onion should be added. For about 5 minutes, cook the onion while frequently stirring. Add the tomatoes and simmer for a further 5 minutes or so, until they are slightly soft.

- Cilantro, garlic, cumin, and chili powder should be added. Stirring often, sauté the garlic for 30 to 60 seconds or until it begins to smell good.

- Add the rice, beans, lime juice, and about ten twists of black pepper after turning off the heat in the pot. After combining, season to taste with more salt (I generally use 1/4 teaspoon) and black pepper.

- Before stuffing the peppers, drain any extra fluid that has accumulated inside of them. Then stuff each pepper well with the rice mixture (if the peppers were actually large, you should have just the perfect quantity of filling—if you have more, keep it to serve as a side dish). Cheese is placed on top of the peppers.
- Bake the cheese for 12 to 13 minutes at 425 degrees, or until it begins to turn brown. Serve warm and sprinkle with fresh cilantro leaves or other desired toppings. For up to 4 days, leftovers store well in the refrigerator, covered. Although I haven't tried it, I think they would freeze well for several months.

Buffalo Tempeh Salad

Servings : 1

21 grams Protein

24 grams Carb

17 grams Fat

311 Cal Per Serving

Est. Prep Time: 3 mins

Est. Cook Time: 12 mins

Est. Total Time: 15 mins

Ingredients

- 1 block tempeh (about 6 oz)
- Cooking spray (or olive oil)
- 1/3 cup buffalo sauce
- 4 cups greens
- 1 cup chopped cherry tomatoes
- 1/2 a cucumber , sliced
- 1/4 cup diced onion
- 1/2 cup shredded carrots

for the dressing:

- 2 tablespoon tahini

- Juice of 1/2 a lemon (about 1 tablespoon)
- 1/4 teaspoon garlic powder
- Salt and pepper to taste
- Water to thin (I used about 1/4 cup)

Instructions

- A skillet should be heated to medium. Spray with cooking spray once it's heated.
- The tempeh can be cut into whatever shape you like. Although you could also use strips or cubes, I chose to use triangles.
- Add the tempeh to the pan and heat for 2 minutes, or until browned on one side. Once flipped, heat for a further 2 minutes, or until the second side is browned.
- Stir in the buffalo sauce after adding it. Cook the tempeh for an additional

minute to thoroughly coat it with the buffalo sauce. Place aside.

- Put the salads together. Place half of the greens into two bowls. Half of the remaining ingredients should be added on top, followed by half of the tempeh.
- The dressing components should be thoroughly combined in a whisk. Enjoy! Drizzle over the salads.

Homemade ricotta gnocchi

Servings : 3

25.9 grams Protein

36 grams Carb

24 grams Fat

462 Cal Per Serving

Est. Prep Time: 30 mins

Est. Cook Time: 15 mins

Est. Total Time: 45 mins

Ingredients

- 250 g ricotta cheese
- 80g finely grated vegetarian parmesan-style cheese
- 2 eggs
- 120 g plain flour (plus more for dusting)
- Salt
- Black pepper
- 1 tablespoon butter + 1 tablespoon oil for frying

Instructions

- In a bowl, combine the eggs, ricotta cheese, and parmesan. Stir well. Mix once more to blend the flour, a dash of salt, and pepper into a soft dough. Add one more tablespoon of flour if the dough appears to be too wet.

- Onto a freshly-floured work surface, spread the dough out. The dough should be formed into a ball and then flattened using a little bit more flour. Cut the disc into halves, then cut each quarter in half again (don't worry about being too precise), to split the mixture into 8 evenly sized pieces.

- In order to prevent it from sticking, roll each piece of dough into a thin snake shape before cutting it into pieces. It doesn't matter how big they are; mine were around 2 cm long.

- Dumplings are placed in a large pan of boiling water. Cook the dumplings for 1-2 minutes or until they float to the top of the water, then use a slotted spoon to extract them.
- To prevent the gnocchi from sticking, a large frying pan should be heated with butter and oil before adding the dumplings. Avoid overcrowding the pan; if necessary, fry them in batches.
- In a bowl, combine the eggs, ricotta cheese, and parmesan. Stir well. Mix once more to blend the flour, a dash of salt, and pepper into a soft dough. Add one more tablespoon of flour if the dough appears to be too wet.
- Onto a freshly-floured work surface, spread the dough out. The dough should be formed into a ball and then flattened using a little bit more flour. Cut the disc

into halves, then cut each quarter in half again (don't worry about being too precise), to split the mixture into 8 evenly sized pieces.

- In order to prevent it from sticking, roll each piece of dough into a thin snake shape before cutting it into pieces. It doesn't matter how big they are; mine were around 2 cm long.
- Dumplings are placed in a large pan of boiling water. Cook the dumplings for 1-2 minutes or until they float to the top of the water, then use a slotted spoon to extract them.
- To prevent the gnocchi from sticking, a large frying pan should be heated with butter and oil before adding the dumplings. Avoid overcrowding the pan; if necessary, fry them in batches.

- Ricotta gnocchi are a little more delicate than potato gnocchi, so be gentle! Cook over medium heat for a few minutes until golden brown and crispy underneath, then carefully turn the dumplings over to cook the other side.
- Add your preferred sauce when the ricotta gnocchi are crisp, then serve right away. I accompanied mine with basil pesto and mushrooms sautéed in garlic.

Overnight Breakfast Casserole With Bacon
And Sweet Potatoes

Servings : 8

18 grams Protein

15 grams Carb

23 grams Fat

348 Cal Per Serving

Est. Prep Time: 25 mins

Est. Cook Time: 55 mins

Est. Total Time: 80 mins

Ingredients

- 8 slices bacon
- 3 cups sweet potato peeled and shredded (on a box grater)
- 3 bell peppers diced
- 3 jalapenos seeds removed and finely diced
- 1 ½ cup cheddar cheese shredded
- 12 eggs
- 1 cup milk

- ½ teaspoon salt
- 1 teaspoon chili powder
- 1 teaspoon ground cumin

Instructions

- Oven should be heated to 375 degrees Fahrenheit. Spray oil in a big casserole dish (8 or 9 x 13) and set it aside.
- Cook the bacon and let it cool a little. Divide into parts.
- After beating the eggs, add the milk, salt, and spices.
- The casserole dish should now contain the bacon, vegetables, and one cup of cheese. Next, pour the egg mixture on top. The remaining cheese should be added after stirring everything.
- You may either bake right away or cover and refrigerate for the night.

- 45 to 60 minutes of baking (mine was ready in 55 minutes). When the casserole is done, the middle will no longer jiggle and will gently rise.
- By inserting a knife or making sure it has reached 160°F on an instant-read thermometer, double check that the middle is done.
- Before serving, let the dish rest for ten minutes.

Kidney Bean Curry (Jamaican-Style)

Servings :4

11 grams Protein

34 grams Carb

4 grams Fat

211 Cal Per Serving

Est. Prep Time: 20 mins

Est. Cook Time: 65 mins

Est. Total Time: 85 mins

Ingredients

- 1 cup dried kidney beans, or 2 (15-ounces) cans rinsed and drained
- 1 tablespoon coconut oil, or 1/4 vegetable broth if oil-free
- 1 small onion, chopped
- 4 cloves garlic, minced
- 1 teaspoon fresh ginger, grated
- 2 stalks green onions, chopped
- 2 medium tomatoes, chopped
- 1 teaspoon ground coriander

- 1/4 teaspoon cumin powder
- 1/4 teaspoon turmeric powder
- 2 sprigs of fresh thyme, or 1/2 teaspoon dried
- 1 cup coconut milk
- 1/4 Cup water
- 1 Scotch Bonnet pepper, or 1/4 teaspoon cayenne pepper
- 1/2 teaspoon salt, Or to taste

Instructions

- If using dried kidney beans, sort and thoroughly rinse them before putting them in a big basin or pot. Soak the beans overnight or for about 8 hours, covering them with water (about 3 cups).
- After washing and drained, add beans to a big pot with enough water to cover (approximately 6 cups) and bring to a boil. Once the beans are ready, turn down

the heat and let them simmer for about an hour.

- After draining the beans, put aside 1/2 cup of the cooking liquid. Oil is heated in a big pot over medium-high heat.
- Add the onion and simmer for four minutes, or until tender. Stir in the ginger and garlic for 30 seconds. Stir for 2 minutes after adding the tomatoes, coriander, cumin, turmeric, and thyme.
- Add the Scotch Bonnet pepper, beans, coconut milk, water, or the reserved liquid, and bring to a boil. Reduce the heat and simmer for about 15 minutes, or until the sauce thickens.
- To taste, add salt.

Chickpea Noodle Soup

Servings :4

12.9 grams Protein

50.7 grams Carb

12 grams Fat

352 Cal Per Serving

Est. Prep Time: 10 mins

Est. Cook Time: 35 mins

Est. Total Time: 45 mins

Ingredients

- 2 Tbsp olive oil or avocado oil
- 1/2 medium white or yellow onion, diced
- 3 cloves garlic, minced
- 5 medium carrots, scrubbed clean and sliced into 1/4-inch rounds
- 4 stalks celery, diced
- 1/4 tsp each sea salt and black pepper
- 7-8 cups vegetable broth
- 1 (15-ounce) can chickpeas, well rinsed and drained

- 4 sprigs thyme
- 1 bay leaf
- 8 ounces vegan-friendly pasta noodles

Instructions

- A big pot should be heated at medium heat. When oil is hot, add onions and cook for five minutes while turning often.
- Saute for 2 minutes more after adding the garlic. Carrots, celery, salt, and pepper are then added. To blend, stir.
- Stirring occasionally, cook for five minutes with lid on. Add the drained, rinsed chickpeas, thyme, and bay leaf after adding the broth (beginning with a smaller amount). a low boil is reached.
- Noodles should be added and broken into bite-sized pieces. Stir to separate, then stir once or twice more as you cook to keep them from sticking.

- Noodles should soften after about 10 minutes; at this point, lower heat to a very low simmer and cover. To combine the flavors, simmer for a further 20 minutes.
- Add more salt or pepper to taste and taste again before making any seasoning adjustments. Serve the dish alone or with rustic bread after removing the bay leaf and thyme sprigs. A decorative garnish is made of thyme leaves or fresh parsley.
- Leftovers can be frozen for up to a month once they have cooled and are covered.

High Protein Greek Yogurt Pasta Sauce

Servings : 4

21 grams Protein

47 grams Carb

17 grams Fat

418 Cal Per Serving

Est. Prep Time: 20 mins

Est. Cook Time: 20 mins

Est. Total Time: 40 mins

Ingredients

- 12 ounces spaghetti
- 3 tablespoons olive oil, divided
- 1 large yellow onion, thinly sliced
- 1 can (15 ounces) chickpeas, rinsed and drained
- 1 cup prepared lentils
- 4 cloves garlic, minced
- 1-1/2 cups full fat Greek yogurt
- 1/4 cup whole milk
- Zest of 1/2 lemon

- 1 teaspoon kosher salt
- 1/2 teaspoon ground black pepper
- 1/4 cup chopped fresh mint
- Red pepper flakes, for serving

Instructions

- big saucepan of salted water over high heat until it boils. Cook the pasta as directed on the package after adding it. After draining the pasta, save 1/4 cup of the cooking water.
- Meanwhile, heat 2 tablespoons oil over medium-high heat in a large, high-sided skillet. Onion should be added and cooked for 8 to 10 minutes, stirring constantly, until dark golden brown. Stirring constantly, cook the chickpeas and lentils for 2 minutes. Place the chickpea mixture in a medium bowl and cover to maintain warmth.

- In the same skillet, warm the final tablespoon of oil slowly over low heat. Add the garlic and stir continuously for 1 minute. Add yogurt, milk, lemon zest, salt, and black pepper after whisking. Cook for 2 minutes while whisking continuously until well warmed.
- Toss together drained pasta with 2 tablespoons of pasta water and yogurt mixture.
- If the sauce is too thick, add a tablespoon of extra pasta water at a time until the appropriate consistency is reached. Pasta should be divided among 4 bowls. Split the chickpea mixture among the pasta. If preferred, garnish with fresh mint and red pepper flakes before serving.

Halloumi Burrito Bowl With Roasted Potatoes

Servings : 4

14.3 grams Protein

57.3 grams Carb

36.8 grams Fat

592 Cal Per Serving

Est. Prep Time: 20 mins

Est. Cook Time: 20 mins

Est. Total Time: 40 mins

Ingredients

- ¼ pound yukon gold potatoes, or something similar
- 2 teaspoons olive oil
- ½ teaspoon smoked paprika
- ¼ teaspoon ground cumin
- ¼ teaspoon salt
- 1 ripe avocado
- 3 tablespoons minced cilantro, plus extra for topping

- 1 tablespoon lime juice
- ¼ teaspoon salt
- 1 tablespoon olive oil
- 2 ounces halloumi cheese
- 1 ½ cups cooked brown rice
- 3 tablespoons toasted pepitas
- Hot Sauce, for topping

Instructions

- Toaster oven: 425 °F. Cut the potato into wedges or 14" cubes, whichever is larger. Add salt, cumin, smoked paprika, and olive oil before tossing. 20 to 25 minutes of roasting should result in light browning of the potatoes.
- Remove the pit from the avocado and scoop out the avocado while the potatoes are roasting. Combine with cilantro, lime juice, and salt in a bowl and mash.
- Over medium-low heat, warm a medium pan. Add the halloumi next, then the

olive oil. Halloumi should be fried until golden on both sides.

- Divide the rice between two bowls, then garnish with the fried halloumi, pepitas, guacamole, and roasted potatoes as preferred. Before serving, garnish with cilantro and pepitas.

Savory Oatmeal

Servings : 4

17 grams Protein

29 grams Carb

16 grams Fat

365 Cal Per Serving

Est. Prep Time: 10 mins

Est. Cook Time: 20 mins

Est. Total Time: 30 mins

Ingredients

- 2 teaspoons olive oil
- 1 tablespoon minced onion
- 1 teaspoon minced garlic
- 1.5 cups rolled oats
- 1 cup beef broth
- 2 cups water
- 1 tablespoon maple syrup
- Mushrooms + Topping
- 1 tablespoon olive oil
- 8 oz. white mushrooms sliced

- 1 tablespoon minced onion
- 1/8 teaspoon salt
- 3 sage leaves
- 4 large eggs
- 1/4 cup raw pepitas or any kind of nut
- 1/4 cup goat cheese crumbles or Boursin

Instructions

- A medium saucepan should have olive oil at the bottom of it. Over medium-high or heat, heat. Add onion and garlic once the olive oil has become aromatic. Cook for two minutes.
- Then add rolled oats and toast for 2 minutes on medium heat. Finally, add water, maple syrup, and beef broth and keep heating over medium-low heat. Cook for approximately 10 minutes, stirring occasionally, until thickened.

- Prepare the mushroom topping while the oatmeal is thickening. Over medium-high heat, warm the olive oil in a medium saucepan. Add three sage leaves, an onion, mushrooms, and salt. The mushrooms should be cooked down in the skillet for 8 to 10 minutes.
- Remove the mushroom topping, discard the sage, and set everything else aside.
- If more oil is required, add it to the same pan and fry four big eggs until the yolks are the correct consistency.
- Serve the goat cheese, pepitas, sauteed mushrooms, and fried egg on top of the savory oatmeal.

Spicy Black Bean Burger

Servings :

32.1 grams Protein

91 grams Carb

22.2 grams Fat

674 Cal Per Serving

Est. Prep Time: 10 mins

Est. Cook Time: 20 mins

Est. Total Time: 30 mins

Ingredients

- 15 oz. Black Beans
- 2 Whole Burger Buns
- 1 Red Bell Pepper
- 1 Yellow Onion
- 1/2 cup Fresh Cilantro
- 1/2 cup Italian Breadcrumbs
- 1/2 cup Grated Parmesan Cheese
- 1 tbsp. Minced Garlic
- 1 Large Organic Egg
- 2 Provolone Cheese Slices

Burger Seasonings:

- 1 tsp. Oregano
- 1/2 tsp. Black Pepper
- 1/2 tsp. Garlic Powder
- 1/2 tsp. Paprika
- 1/2 tsp. Chili Powder
- 1/4 tsp. Adobo All-Purpose Seasoning
- 1/4 tsp. Crushed Red Pepper Flakes
- Dash Ground Cayenne Red Pepper

Avocado Sauce:

- 1 Medium Avocado
- 1/4 cup Mayo
- 1 tsp. Lemon Juice
- 1 tbsp. Parsley Flakes
- 1/2 tsp. Minced Garlic
- 1/2 tsp. Black Pepper
- 1/4 tsp. Himalayan Salt

Instructions

- Allow canned black beans to drain and settle for ten to fifteen minutes. Mash black beans with a fork or potato masher in a big basin after adding them. Placed aside.
- Your red bell pepper and onion should be cut into large pieces and added to a food processor to be chopped finely. Add any extra liquid to the same bowl as the beans after draining it.
- Then combine all of the remaining burger ingredients and seasonings. Cover and chill for 30 minutes.
- Create patties out of the bean mixture, then cook them for 5 minutes on each side, adding a slice of cheese after the first flip.
- Remove the avocado's seed and skin to make the sauce. Blend in the ingredients for the avocado sauce.

- Add lettuce, tomatoes, and avocado sauce to create your burger.

Mapo Tofu

Servings : 4

11.2 grams Protein

9.3 grams Carb

18 grams Fat

227 Cal Per Serving

Est. Prep Time: 15 mins

Est. Cook Time: 15 mins

Est. Total Time: 30 mins

Ingredients

- 1 pound (455g) soft or silken tofu,
- 8 cups (1.9L) water
- 2 teaspoons (12g) table or sea salt
- Mushrooms
- 1 tablespoon neutral oil (vegetable, canola, safflower, etc.)
- 1 cup (65g) finely diced shiitake mushrooms
- Sauce
- 3 to 4 teaspoons peppercorn

- 1 teaspoon (12g) cornstarch or tapioca starch
- 1/2 cup (118ml) water
- 2 tablespoons of neutral oil (vegetable, canola, safflower, etc.)
- 2 tablespoons (15g) minced garlic
- 1 tablespoon (7g) minced ginger
- 2 tablespoons (40g) doubanjiang
- 1 1/2 tablespoons (10g) gochugaru,
- 1/2 teaspoon (2g) sugar
- 1 stalk of scallions, sliced, lighter pieces and dark green pieces separated
- drizzle of sesame oil

Instructions

- Drain the tofu block, then take it out of the packaging. Tofu should be cut into 3/4-inch chunks.

- Bring to a boil 8 cups of water with 2 tablespoons of salt in a saucepan. Remove the pot from the heat.
- Tofu cubes should be carefully lowered into the hot water using a skimmer or slotted spoon. As you make the sauce, leave the tofu to soak in hot water.
- Prepare mushrooms
- In a wok, heat 1 tablespoon of oil over medium-high heat. While regularly stirring, add the mushrooms and simmer for about 2 minutes.
- After removing the mushrooms from the heat, place them in a basin.
- Make the sauce.
- Utilizing a mortar and pestle or spice grinder, ground the Sichuan peppercorns.
- The stiff husks should be removed by sifting the powdered peppercorns

through a fine sieve. Toss the brittle husks out .

- Stir together 1 teaspoon cornstarch and 1/2 cup water in a small bowl. Discard it.
- 2 tablespoons of oil are warmed up over a medium-high flame. 30 seconds later, add the ginger and garlic and sauté them. The doubanjiang should then be added and sautéed for an additional 30 seconds. Gochugaru (or other chili flakes) and sugar should be added, then whisk everything together. Once more whisk the cornstarch slurry and add to the wok to complete the process. Don't forget to include the scallion's white and light green sections. For 2 minutes, let the sauce simmer.
- Add sauce to the mushrooms and tofu.
- Wok with the mushrooms that have been sautéed. Transfer the warmed tofu to the

wok as well using a skimmer or a slotted spoon. After that, thoroughly combine everything. Be careful since the tofu is easily broken apart and is quite delicate.

- A serving bowl should now contain the mapo tofu.
- Over the tofu, drizzle a tiny quantity of sesame oil. Use the scallion's dark green bits to garnish the tofu. Serve with brown or jasmine rice.

Rican Rice and Beans

Servings : 6

13.1 grams Protein

68.2 grams Carb

2.9 grams Fat

344 Cal Per Serving

Est. Prep Time: 6 hrs

Est. Cook Time: 2 hrs

Est. Total Time: 8 hrs

Ingredients

- 1 pound dry pinto or pink beans, soaked overnight for 6-8 hours, no longer
- 6-8 cups water or vegetarian broth
- 1-2 bay leaves
- 2 teaspoons olive oil
- ½ cup finely diced yellow onion
- ½ cup finely diced green bell pepper
- ¼ cup finely diced cilantro
- 3 cloves garlic, minced

- 1 cup no salt added tomato sauce (from one 15 oz can -- reserve extra sauce for rice)
- 3 teaspoons (2 packets) Sazon Culantro ey Achiote*
- 2 teaspoons olive oil
- 1/3 cup finely diced yellow onion
- 1/3 cup finely diced green bell pepper
- ¼ cup finely diced cilantro
- 2 cloves garlic, minced
- ½ cup no salt added tomato sauce
- 3 teaspoons (2 packets) Sazon Culantro y Achiote
- ⅛ teaspoon adobo (or just a pinch)
- 1 (15 oz) can Goya Green Pigeon peas*
- 3 cups water
- 2 cups basmati white rice

Instructions

- In 6-8 cups of water or broth, soak the beans and bay leaf for 6–8 hours; the beans should have about 1 inch of liquid on top of them. I advise only soaking your beans for eight hours. You can soak in a warm bath.
- After soaking the beans, bring them to a boil for one to two minutes, then lower the heat, cover the pot, and simmer the beans gently for one to two hours, or until they are soft and tender. When the beans are halfway done cooking, you may start making your sofrito, or you can turn off the heat and let the beans sit while you prepare your sofrito.
- It just depends on your culinary proficiency and preferences. DO NOT DRAIN THE BEANS, BUT REMOVE THE BAY LEAF. In the recipe, the liquid is crucial!

- Making Sofrito (for a pound of beans)
  Sofrito, which translates to sauce in Spanish, is a common ingredient in many of Puerto Rico's key basic cuisines. A medium skillet with oil in it should be heated to medium. Add onion, green pepper, cilantro, and garlic to the heated oil. Cook for 3-5 minutes, or until green peppers are tender and onions are translucent. Sazon and tomato sauce are added, and the heat is reduced to low; the mixture will thicken in about two minutes.
- Remember that you weren't supposed to drain the beans before adding the sofrito, and cook the mixture, covered, over low heat for 20 to 30 minutes while stirring regularly to let the flavors meld. After that, cover the beans to maintain the heat while you finish preparing the rest of the

food. For about an hour, they ought to stay hot enough.

- Make the rice by adding oil to a medium pot and setting it over medium heat while the beans and sofrito are cooking. Add onion, green pepper, cilantro, and garlic to the heated oil. Cook for 3-5 minutes, or until green peppers are tender and onions are translucent.

- Tomato sauce, sazon, and adobo are added to a medium-low heat and simmered for 2 minutes to combine the sauce. Bring to a boil after which add the entire can of pigeon peas (with the liquid; DO NOT DRAIN) and 3 cups of water. Once it boils, add 2 cups of rice and simmer for 20 minutes, covered, over low heat, until the rice is cooked.

- Once the rice and beans are cooked, taste them both and, if necessary, add additional salt.
- Serve the rice and beans in a bowl with any extra bean sauce. Garnish with cilantro and a few slices of avocado. If you like a little spice, you can also add spicy sauce. serving six.

Brown Rice Veggie Bowl With Crispy Tofu

Servings : 4

23 grams Protein

81 grams Carb

24 grams Fat

620 Cal Per Serving

Est. Prep Time: 30 mins

Est. Cook Time:30 mins

Est. Total Time: 60 mins

Ingredients

- 1/3 cup (80 ml) rice vinegar
- ¼ cup (60 ml) tamari
- 2 tablespoons (30 ml) vegetable oil, such as sunflower or grapeseed
- 1-2 teaspoons (more or less, to your taste) Vietnamese chili garlic sauce or Sriracha
- 1 teaspoon granulated garlic
- 1 pound firm or extra firm tofu
- CRISPY COATING:
- ½ cup (60 g) cornstarch

- 1 1/2 teaspoons granulated garlic
- 1 1/2 teaspoons fine sea salt
- 1 teaspoon mild chili powder
- 2-4 tablespoons (30-60 ml) vegetable oil, such as sunflower or grapeseed
- BOWLS:
- 1 recipe roasted delicata squash with miso butter, warm, plus extra miso butter for drizzling
- 1 cup short grain brown rice (covered in cool water and soaked 15-30 minutes)
- salt, as needed
- 4 large eggs
- 1 bunch kale, stems removed and discarded, leaves sliced thinly
- 2-3 teaspoons rice vinegar
- 2 teaspoons toasted sesame oil
- sesame seeds, nori flakes, and togarashi for sprinkling

Instructions

- Stir together the rice vinegar, tamari, chili sauce, and granulated garlic in a sizable, shallow basin or baking dish. To remove the water from the tofu, firmly press it between two layers of paper towels. Then, slice it into bite-sized pieces (I like rectangles roughly the size of my thumb). If you can, arrange the tofu in a single layer and toss with the marinade. Refrigerate, tossing occasionally, for at least one hour and ideally three to four or even overnight.

- In a small bowl, combine the cornstarch, salt, chili powder, and minced garlic to make the tofu coating.

- THE BOWLS SHOULD BE PREPARED WHILE THE TOFU MARINATES:

- If you haven't already, start roasting the delicata squash and preparing the miso butter.
- In the meantime, drain the soaked brown rice and add it to a medium saucepan with a lid. Add 1 34 cups of water and a scant 1/2 teaspoon of fine sea salt or kosher salt to the pan as well. 30 to 45 minutes should pass until the rice is soft and has absorbed all the liquid after bringing to a simmer, covering, and reducing to a bare simmer. If you want the rice to be more soft, test it and add extra water. Allow the rice to sit, covered, for 10 more minutes after you've cooked it to your preference. With a fork, fluff.
- Place a small saucepan with water over high heat and quickly bring to a boil while the rice cooks. One by one, add the eggs.

- Boil the eggs for the desired amount of time: For very runny yolks , cook for 5 minutes, for soft yolks, for 6 minutes, and for custardy yolks, for 7 minutes. To end the cooking, drain the eggs and replenish the pot with cool water. The eggs should be peeled, well cleaned, and set aside after cutting into a tester to check the doneness.
- Combine the kale with the smaller amounts of vinegar and sesame oil in a medium bowl. Season with a few pinches of salt. After tasting, adjust the amount of any ingredient as desired. Hold until required.
- Fry the tofu next. Tofu should be thoroughly drained into a bowl using a sieve.
- In the bowl containing the cornstarch mixture, add a third of the tofu and toss

to coat. In a large skillet over a medium burner, heat 2 tablespoons of the oil until it shimmers. Shake off any extra coating before adding the tofu in one layer. Cook each piece for about a minute on each side, turning when the first side has become golden brown. To drain the tofu, place it on a platter covered with two layers of paper towels. Repeat the process with the remaining tofu, adding extra oil as necessary to the pan.

- Divide the rice among four sizable, shallow bowls and top each with the roasted butternut squash, crispy tofu, a mound of kale, and an egg. Add some miso butter to the bowl and garnish with sesame seeds, nori flakes, and togarashi. At room temperature or heated, serve.

- The bowl's components can be stored in the refrigerator airtight for a few days.

Heat the rice and squash in the oven, toaster oven, or microwave till warm for the ultimate leftovers experience. After crisping up the tofu once more in a small skillet over medium heat, assemble the bowls.

Vegetable Tofu Scramble

Servings : 4

23.38 grams Protein

11.68 grams Carb

16.3 grams Fat

259.68 Cal Per Serving

Est. Prep Time: 15 mins

Est. Cook Time:20 mins

Est. Total Time: 35 mins

Ingredients

- 14 oz. firm or extra firm tofu
- 8 oz. mushrooms
- 2 Tbsp cooking oil
- 1/2 tsp garlic powder
- 1/4 tsp freshly cracked black pepper
- 1 cup frozen onions and peppers*
- 8 oz. frozen spinach
- 2 Tbsp nutritional yeast
- 1/2 tsp salt
- 1/2 cup salsa

Instructions

- If possible, completely freeze the tofu the days before preparing the meal, then defrost it. Although not necessary, it does result in a nicer texture. When you are prepared to prepare the dish, take the tofu out of the packaging and press or squeeze any remaining moisture from it.

- You can wait for about 15 minutes while the moisture is pushed out by using a tofu press or by placing the tofu on a plate, covering it with a cutting board, and then adding something heavy, like a saucepan. When tofu is frozen, it becomes slightly more sponge-like, and I can squeeze or press out the majority of it with just my hands.

- Prepare the mushrooms for cutting while the tofu is pressing.

- After the frozen spinach has thawed, squeeze any extra water out (I just squeeze it in my fist).
- A big skillet with the cooking oil added to it should be heated to medium. When the oil and skillet are heated, tilt the pan to evenly distribute the oil. Add the tofu crumbles to the skillet and top with the pepper and garlic powder. In the hot skillet, sauté the tofu for two to three minutes. If it begins to stick, don't panic; the moisture from the vegetables will help to release it from the skillet's bottom.
- Once the mushrooms are added, continue to sauté them until they are tender. Once the onions and bell peppers are heated through, add the frozen vegetables.
- Then, add the spinach that has been frozen and squeezed, and continue to

sauté until it is once again heated through.

- Salt and nutritional yeast should then be added to season the skillet. Toss until the nutritional yeast is evenly distributed throughout. Taste it, and add more salt if necessary.
- With a few spoonfuls of salsa on top, plate the vegetable tofu scramble and enjoy!

Black-Eyed Pea Fritters

Servings : 6

6 grams Protein

23 grams Carb

1 grams Fat

126 Cal Per Serving

Est. Prep Time: 15 mins

Est. Cook Time:20 mins

Est. Total Time: 35 mins

Ingredients

- 2 cups cooked black-eyed peas, drained
- ½ cup whole cornmeal
- ¼ cup minced sweet or yellow onion (about ¼ a large onion)
- 2 cloves garlic, grated
- 1 tablespoon chopped fresh thyme
- 1 medium-sized hot pepper, minced
- ½ teaspoon coarse salt
- avocado, peanut or coconut oil for frying

Instructions

- Black-eyed peas, cornmeal, onion, hot pepper, thyme, garlic, and salt should all be combined in a big basin to make the batter. All ingredients should be thoroughly combined to make a thick paste.

- Making the patties In the basin, divide the paste into four equal portions. From each piece, roll and form three patties. Fry immediately in a pan or store in the fridge for up to a day on a covered sheet pan.

- Fry the fritters in a pan: 1-2 tablespoons of oil should be heated to medium-high heat in a skillet. The fritters should be fried in batches, 3–4 minutes each side, only flipping once, until golden brown.

- On a platter covered with paper towels, drain the fritters. If necessary, put some salt on top. (I didn't think it was required.) Enjoy warm, hot, or both.

Oven Roasted Broccoli

Servings : 2

32 grams Protein

78 grams Carb

17 grams Fat

562 Cal Per Serving

Est. Prep Time: 10 mins

Est. Cook Time:25 mins

Est. Total Time: 35 mins

Ingredients

- 450 g broccoli
- 1 red onion
- 1 chili pepper (optional)
- 2 tbsp cashews
- 20 g basil, fresh
- 2 clove garlic
- ½ lime
- 1 tsp salt (divided)
- ¼ tsp black pepper

- 265 g lentils, cooked (or canned and drained)
- 57 g halloumi cheese
- ½ tbsp olive oil
- 1 tbsp parsley or dill
- 100 g ciabatta bread

Instructions

- Set the oven's temperature to 430 F/ 220 C.
- The red onion should be cut into four lengthwise slices, and the broccoli should be cut into large florets. If using, thinly slice the chili pepper.
- Basil, garlic, 12 lime juice, 12 tsp salt, and black pepper can all be added to the food processor with the cashews to create a pesto-like texture (not fully smooth). Add extra salt as desired after tasting. Add a little extra water if necessary.

- Place the lentils and, if using, the thinly sliced chili pepper on a baking sheet. Add the halloumi, broccoli florets, and red onion on top.
- Sprinkle the remaining 12 tsp. of salt and black pepper to taste, then drizzle the pesto seasoning over the vegetables. Olive oil should be brushed over the halloumi and broccoli florets.
- The broccoli florets should be soft after 20 minutes in the oven. For 3-5 minutes, or until the vegetables are golden brown, preheat the oven's broiler or grill to its maximum setting.
- Serve right away after adding freshly chopped parsley or dill on top. Serve with ciabatta bread on the side.

Aubergine and Lentil Vegetarian Moussaka

Servings : 2

30 grams Protein

53 grams Carb

12 grams Fat

421 Cal Per Serving

Est. Prep Time: 10 mins

Est. Cook Time: 40 mins

Est. Total Time: 50 mins

Ingredients

- 250 g eggplants (without the base)
- 1 tsp olive oil
- ½ white onion (diced)
- 2 clove garlic (minced)
- 1 tsp oregano, dried
- ½ tsp cinnamon
- 1 bay leaf
- 1 tbsp tomato puree
- 400 g tomatoes, diced (1 can = 400g)
- 225 g lentils (canned or cooked)

- 1 tbsp soy sauce
- 60 ml water
- ¾ tsp salt (plus more for salting eggplants)
- 1 ½ tsp sugar
- 112 g low fat mozzarella (grated)

Instructions

- Set the oven at 200 C, or 400 F.
- Slice the eggplant into 3–5mm thick pieces. Place thereon a baking sheet, then salt. Let it rest.
- Meanwhile, heat the olive oil over medium heat in a large ovenproof skillet (a frying pan, for instance).
- Add the tomato puree, cinnamon powder, oregano, and bay leaf at this time. Combine and heat for one minute.
- Once added, sauté the onion and garlic until tender. Include cooked lentils, diced

tomatoes, soy sauce, water, salt, and sugar. The sauce should be consistent and thick after 8 minutes of simmering after bringing it to a boil. By thoroughly rinsing them in water, the eggplant slices can be cleaned of the salt.

- Put half of the eggplant slices into the sauce, pushing them down so they form a base (their surface shouldn't be visible). The second layer will then be formed by placing the remaining eggplants on top.
- Bake the pan for 25 minutes in the oven. After removing the pan from the oven, top with shredded mozzarella and re-bake for an additional 10 minutes. Turn on the broiler in the final five minutes to brown the top.
- Take out and start serving right away. This can be chilled and then heated in the oven.

Tofu Bolognese

Servings : 2

23 grams Protein

72 grams Carb

11 grams Fat

478 Cal Per Serving

Est. Prep Time: 10 mins

Est. Cook Time: 20 mins

Est. Total Time: 30 mins

Ingredients

- 140 g wholewheat pasta (choose your favorite, wholegrain would be best)
- For the tofu
- 200 g firm tofu
- 1 tsp olive oil

For the sauce

- 1 red onion
- 2 clove garlic
- 1 tsp olive oil
- 425 g tomatoes, diced (~14.5 oz)

- 2 tbsp tomato paste
- 1 handful basil, fresh (or 2 tbsp frozen or dry basil)
- 1 tsp oregano, dried
- 1 tsp maple syrup (or brown sugar)
- Salt and pepper to taste

Instructions

- Follow the pasta cooking directions. Once completed, season to taste with a little oregano, salt, and olive oil.
-
- Tofu can be minced by crumbling it or cutting it into little pieces.
- In a large frying pan, heat the oil to medium heat before adding the tofu. Add some salt, then cook for 15 minutes, or until the outside is crunchy. Don't forget to taste test, be patient, and stir occasionally! Reduce cooking time by

about 3 minutes if you crumbled it. Garlic and onion should be finely diced.

- Onion and garlic are added to a pan with hot oil. For 3 to 4 minutes, sauté. Pour in the tomato paste, basil, maple syrup, salt, and pepper after adding the diced tomatoes. Ladle it out.
- Put some spaghetti on your plate, add the sauce, and then add the tofu after everything is cooked.
- Enjoy!

Vegan Stuffed Peppers

Servings : 2

30 grams Protein

93 grams Carb

18 grams Fat

615 Cal Per Serving

Est. Prep Time: 20 mins

Est. Cook Time: 60 mins

Est. Total Time: 80 mins

Ingredients

- 85 g quinoa (½ cup = 85g)
- 250 ml vegetable broth
- 4 large bell pepper, red (or your favourite colour)
- 1 tbsp fajita mix (or 1/2 tsp cumin, ¼ tsp chili powder, ½ tsp paprika and 1 pinch salt)
- 3 tbsp nutritional yeast (if you don't have it don't worry, if you do – use it!)
- 80 g sweetcorn

- 100 g tempeh (about 3.5oz or 100g)
- 1 tbsp olive oil
- 480 ml tomato passata
- 1 tsp sugar
- 1 tsp salt
- 12 g basil, fresh

Instructions

- In a pot over medium heat, combine the quinoa with twice as much vegetable stock and cook, stirring frequently and thoroughly, until the water has evaporated. The quinoa will puff up after being removed from the heat and covered with a tea towel.
- Dice the tempeh and cook it for ten minutes in boiling water in the meantime. This will get rid of any resentment, but if you're short for time, you can skip this step.

- After that, cook the tempeh for 10 minutes or so in olive oil. Add a tablespoon or two of water along with the spices (or fajita mix).
- Add the nutritional yeast and stir well once the cooking is finished.
- Sweetcorn should be drained and rinsed.
- After cleaning, quickly scrape out the insides of the peppers. Slice a TINY layer of the sticky-out portion off the bottom of the peppers if they cannot stand up on their own. You don't want the contents of the pepper to fall through, so don't take off more than is necessary.
- The tomato passata should be poured onto a baking dish. Combine the basil leaves, sugar, and salt.
- Set the oven to 200 °C or 390 °F.
- In the passata in the oven dish, place the peppers standing upright.

- Each pepper should include a tbsp of quinoa, a tbsp of tempeh, and a tbsp of corn. Squish it all together, then top with a layer of tempeh or any other leftover ingredients.
- Put them down once more.
- Place the tray in the oven and cook at 200°C/390°F for approximately 40 minutes. When done, the peppers should have browned tops and appear tender (a bit wrinkly).
- Serve in dishes with additional sauce poured around the outside and a dollop of sauce placed on top of each pepper. Add some basil leaves as a finishing garnish.

Lentil Tacos

Servings : 2 (3 tacos each)

29 grams Protein

58 grams Carb

29 grams Fat

615 Cal Per Serving

Est. Prep Time: 5 mins

Est. Cook Time: 15 mins

Est. Total Time: 20 mins

Ingredients

- 1 tsp olive oil
- 6 taco shells (store-bought or self-made)
- 1 onion
- 1 clove garlic
- 4 tbsp water
- 1 cup brown lentils, cooked (1 cup = 1 can 400g/14oz wet weight) (alternatively cook 100g dried lentils in veggie broth according to packet instructions)
- 6 tbsp salsa

- 2 tbsp fajita/burrito seasoning (store-bought or self-made)
- 1 ½ cups mixed salad
- ½ cup cherry tomatoes
- 1 cup cheddar cheese, grated

Instructions

- Dice the garlic and onions.
- The onion is added to the hot oil in the frying pan. Cook until soft over medium heat. If they start to get too dry when frying, add a little boiling water.
- Stir thoroughly after adding the garlic and rinsed lentils.
- The fajita seasoning and water should then be added. Keep giving it a good stir.
- The taco shells or wraps can be baked in the meanwhile. Check the instructions on the packet before cooking; they just need 2 to 3 minutes.

- Slice the tomatoes after washing the salad and them.
- It won't take long to cook the lentils until the water has completely evaporated.

Black Bean Burrito Bowl

Servings : 2

28 grams Protein

67 grams Carb

17 grams Fat

516 Cal Per Serving

Est. Prep Time: 5 mins

Est. Cook Time: 15 mins

Est. Total Time: 30 mins

Ingredients

- 110 g low fat Greek Yogurt (or soy yogurt to make it vegan)
- 1 tsp garlic powder
- ½ ripe avocado (sliced)
- 40 g red onion (thinly sliced or julienned)
- 40 g quinoa
- 120 g vegetable broth
- ½ tsp salt
- 170 g black beans (canned)
- 1 tsp vegetable oil

- 200 g firm tofu (cut in 1 inch cubes)
- 125 g pineapple (cut into ½ inch cubes)
- 2 sprigs cilantro/coriander, fresh
- lemon

Adobo sauce

- 120 ml water
- 1 ½ tsp cornstarch
- 1 ½ tsp chipotle or Tabasco sauce
- ½ tsp paprika
- 1 tsp garlic powder
- 1 tsp honey
- ½ tsp salt
- ½ tsp apple vinegar
- 1 tsp tomato paste
- ¼ tsp cumin, ground
- ½ tsp oregano, dried

Instructions

- Quinoa and broth should be combined in a small pot over medium heat. Once it starts to boil, reduce the heat to a simmer and cook the mixture in accordance with the directions on the package until the grains have opened and are done. Add black beans to the quinoa and heat them for the last 3 minutes.

- Add the oil to a medium nonstick pan and heat it to medium-high. Sliced pineapple and tofu should be the size of a finger. Salt is a good seasoning. occasionally throw.

- While this is going on, slice your avocado, thinly slice your onions, chop your cilantro, and make the yogurt sauce by combining yogurt, garlic powder, salt, and pepper to taste. Keep back until required.

- Cold water, cornstarch, chipotle sauce, paprika, garlic powder, honey, salt, apple vinegar, tomato paste, cumin, and oregano should all be combined in a bowl.

- Add the sauce to the pan and turn the heat to low. Tofu and pineapple are combined after the sauce has been cooked until it thickens. Removing the pineapple from the pan will prevent it from becoming sauce-coated.

- With the tofu, black beans, quinoa, pineapple, onions, avocado, and cilantro, plate the burrito bowl. Serve with a lemon wedge and yogurt sauce.

Vegetarian Toad in the Hole

Servings :4

32.1 grams Protein

42.9 grams Carb

21.7 grams Fat

502 Cal Per Serving

Est. Prep Time: 10 mins

Est. Cook Time: 40 mins

Est. Total Time: 50 mins

Ingredients

- 4-6 vegetarian sausages (Beyond Meat or Quorn, for example)
- 2 tbsp vegetable or canola oil
- 1 cup all purpose flour
- 2 eggs
- ¾ cup semi-skimmed milk
- ½ tsp salt

Instructions

- Put the oil and vegetarian sausages in a baking tray and preheat the oven to 200°C (390°F).
- Use a hand blender or electric mixer to combine the eggs, flour, milk, salt, and, if used, mustard, in the interim. Until the following phase, let the batter stand.
- Take the dish out of the oven when the sausages begin to brown, and slowly pour the batter mixture over (but not on top of) the sausages.
- Return it to the oven for a further 25 to 35 minutes, or until it is golden and puffy.
- Done! It's time for your veggie toad in the hole.

Baked Feta with Veggies

Servings : 2

23 grams Protein

58 grams Carb

22 grams Fat

505 Cal Per Serving

Est. Prep Time: 10 mins

Est. Cook Time: 30 mins

Est. Total Time: 40 mins

Ingredients

- ½ cup brown rice (uncooked) (this is optional, and our favorite side)
- 5 oz low fat feta cheese
- 1 tbsp olive oil
- 2 tbsp basil, dried (fresh is fine)
- 2 tbsp parsley, dried (fresh is fine)
- 1 clove garlic
- 1 onion (red or white)
- 1 red bell pepper (your fave colour)
- 2 good handful cherry tomatoes

- 1 chili / jalapeño
- 1 handful olives
- 10 tbsp water
- Salt to taste

Instructions

- Set the oven's temperature to 180 C (360 F).
- According to the directions on the package, prepare the brown rice.
- Lay the cheese on a baking sheet after cutting it into two equal, thin pieces.
- Over the cheese, spread half of the dry herbs.
- All vegetables should be chopped into small bits and thrown into a basin.
- Mix well after adding the oil, salt, water, and the remaining herbs. (If using fresh herbs, add them completely to this mixture to prevent burning.)

- Around the cheese, spread the vegetable mixture.
- Bake the vegetables for 30 minutes, or until tender.
- Serve with hummus and brown rice.
- Done

Beetroot Pasta

Servings : 2

26 grams Protein

87 grams Carb

24 grams Fat

621 Cal Per Serving

Est. Prep Time: 10 mins

Est. Cook Time: 15 mins

Est. Total Time: 25 mins

Ingredients

- 5 oz wholewheat pasta
- 1 tbsp olive oil
- 1 tbsp white wine vinegar
- 1 handful walnuts
- 1 onion
- 1 clove garlic
- 2 tsp sage, fresh (dried is fine too; or rosemary)
- 1 large beetroot, pre-cooked (or two small)

- 3 oz low fat feta cheese
- 1 handful arugula/rocket (1 handful = 50g)
- 1 lemon (sliced)
- Salt and pepper to taste

Instructions

- Cook pasta as directed on the packet.
- In a sizable dry pan over medium heat, toast the walnuts for a few minutes.
- Dice the garlic and onion.
- On low to medium heat, add the onion and garlic to the pan with the olive oil, followed by the walnuts in a small side bowl. Add sage, salt, and pepper after 2 minutes.
- When the beetroot is unwrapped, add the extra liquid to the pan. There ought to be only a few drops. Beetroot should also be cut into small cubes and added.

- Mixture should now contain white wine vinegar.
- Once done, use a colander to drain the pasta and collect the leftover water, saving about half a cup (100 ml).
- Pasta and water should be added to the pan.
- If you purchased the beet juice, it is now time to add the colour. Put it in the mixture. Stir everything thoroughly, then boil for about 6 minutes before tasting.
- Wash and roughly chop the arugula as it simmers.
- Add the arugula, feta, walnuts, and lemon segments as garnish.
- Enjoy!

Heavenly Halloumi Salad

Servings : 3

24 grams Protein

48 grams Carb

22 grams Fat

474 Cal Per Serving

Est. Prep Time: 5 mins

Est. Cook Time: 20 mins

Est. Total Time: 25 mins

Ingredients

- ⅔ cup quinoa
- ½ tsp salt (for the quinoa)
- For the dressing and salad:
-
- 1 tbsp olive oil
- 1 can chickpeas (drained and rinsed)
- 2 cups arugula (rocket)
- 1 tsp sweet paprika
- 1 lime (juiced and zested)

Instructions

- Salt the quinoa as directed on the packet before cooking it. Using twice as much water as quinoa and cooking it until the water has evaporated is what we've found to work best. Turn off the heat and wait five minutes while covered with a tea towel.

- Drain and rinse the chickpeas in the interim. Shake and give the rocket/arugula a short wash. Place them in a large basin.

- Lime juice and zest are combined with olive oil. Including the sweet paprika

- Halloumi should be chopped into bite-sized pieces and fried for two to three minutes on each side.

- Combine the cooked quinoa with the chickpeas, rocket, and arugula when it is done. Add the lime-oil mixture and stir. Serve the halloumi on top in bowls. Enjoy!

Cheese and Spinach Pie

Servings : 2

24 grams Protein

43 grams Carb

21 grams Fat

449 Cal Per Serving

Est. Prep Time: 5 mins

Est. Cook Time: 35 mins

Est. Total Time: 40 mins

Ingredients

- 14 oz potato
- 1 tsp olive oil
- Salt to taste
- 3 eggs
- ½ tsp garlic powder (or garlic salt)
- ½ tsp nutmeg
- 1 tsp onion powder
- 2 oz cheddar cheese
- 2 oz low fat cottage cheese
- 2 oz spinach (if frozen, let defrost)

- 1 tomatoes
- 1 tsp basil, dried
- 1 tsp oregano, dried
- Salt and pepper to taste
- 1 tsp olive oil

Instructions

- Set the oven to 200 °C or 390 °F.
- Add salt and olive oil after chopping the potatoes into small (about thumb-sized) pieces. Position on a tray.
- Eggs should be beaten in a big bowl.
- Add the salt, pepper, nutmeg, onion powder, and garlic.
- Activate the cottage cheese and cheddar cheese. Stir everything together before adding the spinach.
- Make sure the egg and spice mixture is well coated on everything.

- Pour into a 4-inch pie pan that has been lightly greased, then smooth it out evenly.
- The tomato slices.
- Along with the potatoes on the side, it is placed in the oven. After 15 minutes of baking, remove the pie from the oven and cover it with the tomatoes. Toss the potatoes quickly.
- Cook for a further 15 to 20 minutes.
- When ready, top with a little extra salt, pepper, basil, and oregano.
- Done! Enjoy eating the pie with the potatoes on the side!

Flawless Feta and Spinach Pancakes

Servings : 2

29 grams Protein

49 grams Carb

19 grams Fat

459 Cal Per Serving

Est. Prep Time: 10 mins

Est. Cook Time: 20 mins

Est. Total Time: 30 mins

Ingredients

- 1 tsp olive oil
- 1 small onion
- 2 cloves garlic
- 12.5 oz spinach (frozen)
- ¾ cup wholegrain flour
- 2 eggs
- ¾ cup milk of choice
- 2 tsp olive oil
- Salt to taste

Instructions

- Grab a pot and heat it on medium with some olive oil, minced onion, and minced garlic.
- spinach is now added. To quickly defrost, stir it occasionally. To taste, add some salt.
- Until the pancakes are done, simmer. Blend the spinach until it becomes "saucy" if it has not previously been finely diced.
- Ideally using a hand blender, combine the flour, eggs, milk, and a pinch of salt in a bowl. Verify that there are no lumps. If the batter is still too "doughy," add more milk. The batter should be liquidy.
- Pour the pancake batter into a pan after adding some olive oil. Fry each side for

three to four minutes. You'll quickly get the hang of it.

Vegan Chickpea Winter Salad

Servings : 2

17 grams Protein

49 grams Carb

18 grams Fat

398 Cal Per Serving

Est. Prep Time: 10 mins

Est. Cook Time: 20 mins

Est. Total Time: 30 mins

Ingredients

- 1 can chickpeas (1 can = 15.5 oz)
- 1 bunch parsley, fresh
- 1 lime (zested and juiced)
- 1 beetroot, pre-cooked
- 2 tbsp mixed seeds (eg. pumpkin & sunflower seeds)
- 1 orange (sliced in filets)
- 1 tsp hot sauce (eg. sriracha)
- 1 clove garlic
- 4 tsp olive oil

- 1 tbsp water
- Salt and pepper to taste

Instructions

- The chickpeas should be drained and thoroughly rinsed. The seeds should be aromatic after being heated on medium (no oil needed).
- Parsley should be chopped and added to a food processor or mortar. Blend in the garlic, spicy sauce, olive oil, salt, and pepper after adding the lime zest and juice.
- Add the "parsley dip" to the chickpeas in a bowl. Put it on a platter after giving it a thorough toss and seasoning it with salt to taste.
- Filet the orange (this video is great; after peeling it, simply slice the orange), dice

the beetroot, and add garnish to the salad.

- Add some capers if you'd like, sprinkle the seeds on top, and savor.

Smoked Tofu & Hummus Buddha Bowl

Servings : 2

21 grams Protein

52 grams Carb

16 grams Fat

426 Cal Per Serving

Est. Prep Time: 5 mins

Est. Cook Time: 10 mins

Est. Total Time: 15 mins

Ingredients

- ½ tsp turmeric
- 100 g basmati rice
- 300 g smoked tofu
- 2 tsp olive oil
- 2 handful lamb's lettuce
- 1 small red onion
- 4 tbsp hummus
- 1 tbsp lemon juice
- 6 tbsp water
- ½ tsp salt

Instructions

- Follow the directions on the rice package for preparation. Salt and turmeric should be combined. You are aware that the rice to water ratio is 1:2. Use cold water, bring to a boil, and then cover and simmer for ten minutes. Done

- Cut up the smoked tofu. After that, add some olive oil to a skillet and add the tofu that has been diced. around 7 minutes to fry.

- Clean the lamb's lettuce, then slice the red onion very thinly. After that, add both to your bowl.

- Add the hummus, lemon juice, and water to a small bowl. Mix well.

- Time to assemble: fill your bowl with the cooked rice and fried tofu. The hummus dressing should now be applied. Adding salt is optional.

- Enjoy!

Healthy Egg Salad

Servings : 2

24 grams Protein

39 grams Carb

22 grams Fat

446 Cal Per Serving

Est. Prep Time: 5 mins

Est. Cook Time: 15 mins

Est. Total Time: 20 mins

Ingredients

- 85 g quinoa
- 4 eggs
- 45 g beets (thinly sliced into semi circles, about ½ a beetroot, pre-cooked works too)
- 3 tbsp white vinegar
- 120 g salad greens
- 1 tbsp olive oil
- ½ tbsp honey
- 1 tsp apple vinegar

- ¼ tsp salt
- 60 g low fat feta cheese or low fat goats cheese (crumbled)
- 1 handful parsley, fresh
- Black pepper to taste

Instructions

- To prepare the quinoa, follow the directions on the packet. 2 parts water are combined with 1 part quinoa. When the water has evaporated, bring to a boil, reduce heat, cover with a tea towel for about five minutes, and then remove from heat.
- Add the eggs to a small pot of boiling water. Cook for 6 minutes and 30 seconds for a jammy egg with slightly liquid yolk in the centre or 7 minutes for a firmer yet still jammy egg. Take the

eggs out and chill them in ice water. Peel them when they're cool.

- Beets should be thinly sliced and placed in a small kettle with water. The water should come halfway up the beets. Add the white vinegar and two generous pinches of salt.
- Let the liquid simmer for 3 minutes after it comes to a boil. Remove the beets from the heated liquid right away. When using beets that have already been boiled, slice them and let them sit in the same quantity of hot water and vinegar.
- White vinegar with 45 grams of beets
- Combine 1/4 teaspoon salt, apple vinegar, honey, and olive oil.
- 1 tbsp olive oil, ½ tbsp honey, 1 tsp apple vinegar, ¼ tsp salt\sPlate the salad with the salad greens, beets, crumbled cheese, parsley leaves and eggs cut in half or

fourths. Add a generous amount of salt and black pepper to the ingredients. Add the dressing to the dish to finish it.

Homemade Ramen in a Jar

Servings : 2

24 grams Protein

39 grams Carb

22 grams Fat

414 Cal Per Serving

Est. Prep Time: 15 mins

Est. Cook Time: 5 mins

Est. Total Time: 20 mins

Ingredients

- 1 egg
- 1 vegetable broth cube (enough for 4 cups water)
- 2 tsp red curry paste
- 2 tsp sesame oil
- 4 tbsp soy sauce
- 1 clove garlic (minced)
- 2 tsp sugar
- 2 tsp lemon juice
- 70 g rice noodles

- 130 g edamame (soy beans) (shelled, precooked or cooked)
- 200 g firm tofu (cut into 1 inch cubes)
- 1 medium carrot (grated)
- 2 spring onions (sliced)
- 2 handful cilantro/coriander, fresh
- 2 tsp sesame seeds
- 900 ml water

Instructions

- For more specific directions, please refer to the recipe notes.
- In a pot of boiling water, boil an egg for 7 minutes. Remove heat immediately, then plunge under cold water to totally cool. Peel, then split in half.
- Prepare the chopped cilantro leaves, minced garlic, cubed tofu, shaved or shredded carrots, and sliced spring onions.

- In the meantime, combine half of the vegetable stock cube, red curry paste, sesame oil, soy sauce, minced garlic, sugar, and lemon juice in each of the two mason jars. Mix everything together completely.
- Rice noodles, edamame beans, cubed tofu, carrot, half an egg per serving, spring onions, cilantro leaves, and sesame seeds are added in layers. The jar should be covered with a lid and kept cool until it is time to consume.
- Add 2 cups of boiling water per serving to the jar when you're ready to eat. For a steaming hot soup, let stand for one or two minutes and then ideally microwave for another two to three minutes. Add salt, then relish!

Vegetarian Banh Mi

Servings : 2

20 grams Protein

48 grams Carb

19 grams Fat

432 Cal Per Serving

Est. Prep Time: 15 mins

Est. Cook Time: 15 mins

Est. Total Time: 30 mins

Ingredients

- 65 g carrot, grated (or julienned)
- ½ cucumber
- ½ tsp honey
- ½ tbsp apple vinegar
- 2 tbsp low fat Greek Yogurt
- 2 tbsp mayonnaise
- ½ tsp salt
- 15 g cilantro/coriander, fresh (separated from stalks)
- 190 g brown lentils, cooked

- 1 egg
- 40 g panko style breadcrumbs
- ½ tsp garlic powder
- ½ tsp paprika
- ¼ tsp black pepper
- ½ tbsp olive oil
- ½ chili / jalapeño (optional)
- 2 wholegrain baguettes (individual baguettes)

Instructions

- The julienned carrots, cucumber slices, apple cider vinegar, honey, and half of the salt should all be combined in a small bowl. Combine and let sit until required.
- Blend Greek yogurt, mayonnaise, half a cup of cilantro leaves, and salt. Add a teaspoon of water if necessary. till you need to, rest.

- Create a smooth purée in the food processor using the egg and lentils. Transfer the purée to a medium bowl and stir in the panko breadcrumbs, paprika, garlic powder, black pepper, and 1/2 teaspoon of salt. Until the dough is uniform, combine with your hands. Create 6 smaller or 4 larger patties out of the dough.
- Olive oil is added to a non-stick pan that has been heated to a high temperature. When the patties are finished, they should be a lovely golden brown hue.
- Open the baguettes, then apply the green sauce on both sides. Add the remaining cilantro leaves, carrots, cucumbers, sliced chilies, and lentil patties to fill (if using). Enjoy.

Spinach Tomato Quesadillas

Servings : 2

28 grams Protein

30 grams Carb

26 grams Fat

458 Cal Per Serving

Est. Prep Time: 5 mins

Est. Cook Time: 10 mins

Est. Total Time: 15 mins

Ingredients

- 1 large tomato (sliced)
- 80 g spinach
- 1 tbsp pesto (make sure it's the vegetarian kind)
- 30 g cheddar cheese (sliced)
- 125 g low fat mozzarella (1 ball = 125g/4.5oz)
- 2 wholegrain tortillas

Instructions

- Grab a tortilla and cover half of it with a coating of pesto. You can also create your own.
- Put a thin layer of cheese slices on top (mixing the cheddar and mozzarella together).
- Sliced tomato, spinach, and additional cheese are then added on top.
- Place the tortilla in a pan and fold the top half over.
- Approximately four minutes on medium heat. If you'd like the quesadilla to flatten out properly, you can put a saucepan on top of it.
- When the cheese has melted, flip the pan over and cook for a further 4 minutes.
- Munch.

Vegetarian Greek Pitas

Servings : 2

25 grams Protein

80 grams Carb

15 grams Fat

520 Cal Per Serving

Est. Prep Time: 8 mins

Est. Cook Time: 2 mins

Est. Total Time: 10 mins

Ingredients

- ½ red onion
- 1 small cucumber
- 150 g cherry tomatoes
- 85 g low fat feta cheese (use regular if you prefer)
- 4 pitas (we like wholegrain)
- 1 handful spinach
- 4 tbsp hummus (to spread)
- ½ lemon (juiced)
- 1 tbsp oregano, fresh (1 tbsp = 1 tsp dried)

- 1 tsp red pepper flakes (dried cayenne also goes really well)
- 2 tsp olive oil
- 1 tbsp red wine vinegar (balsamic vinegar or any you have is also great!)
- salt

Instructions

- Cucumber, tomato, onion, and cheese should be chopped and placed in a bowl.

Separately, in a bowl:

- Add the lemon juice, vinegar, and olive oil.
- Add the salt, pepper, and oregano.
- Mix thoroughly, then pour over salad. Toss it in the air
- Toast the pitas before filling with hummus.
- Enjoy!

Chickpea Salad Sandwich

Servings : 6

23 grams Protein

61 grams Carb

6 grams Fat

432 Cal Per Serving

Est. Prep Time: 10 mins

Est. Cook Time: 10 mins

Est. Total Time: 20 mins

Ingredients

- 795 g chickpeas, cooked
- 7.5 tbsp Greek yogurt (~2%)
- 7.5 tbsp low fat cottage cheese
- 6 sprigs dill, fresh
- 3 tsp onion powder
- 4.5 tbsp capers
- 3 tbsp water
- 1.5 tsp salt
- 84 g baby spinach
- 6 radishes

- 1140 g wholegrain bread (or ciabatta/baguette)

Instructions

- Add the chickpeas, Greek yogurt, cottage cheese, dill leaves, onion powder, capers, water, and salt to the food processor's bowl. Process until the mixture is semi-smooth and contains some little chickpea bits. If required, taste and add additional salt.
- Cut up radishes.
- Toast the bread if you'd like to make two meals out of it.
- Sliced radish, baby spinach, and chickpea salad should be spread on bread.

Vegetarian Wedge Salad

Servings : 2

23 grams Protein

55 grams Carb

13 grams Fat

401 Cal Per Serving

Est. Prep Time: 12 mins

Est. Cook Time: 8 mins

Est. Total Time: 20 mins

Ingredients

- 60 g quinoa (uncooked)
- 4 tbsp cashews
- 170 g Greek yogurt (2%)
- 2 tbsp nutritional yeast
- 1 tsp onion powder
- 0.25 tsp garlic powder
- 1 tsp oregano, dried
- 0.5 tsp salt
- 0.5 tsp sugar
- 2 tbsp chives (chopped)

- 150 g corn, cooked (yellow or white, 140 g)
- 85 g cherry tomatoes (halved)
- 1 iceberg lettuce

Instructions

- For 8–10 minutes, or until the grains puff and are completely cooked, boil the quinoa in a small pot of salted water. Drain and reserve next.
- In the meantime, add the cashews, yogurt, nutritional yeast, onion, garlic, dried oregano, salt, sugar, and 1/4 cup of water to the food processor. Process until dressing is smooth and creamy. When the dressing has reached the ideal thickness for you, if it is still too thick, add a little bit more water.
- Prepare iceberg lettuce wedges, cherry tomatoes cut in half, and chives.

- Place the lettuce wedges on a platter and season with salt if you plan to eat them right away. After dressinging the wedges, add the quinoa, corn, tomatoes, and chives.
- If using a mason jar, layer the ingredients in two large mason jars as follows: dressing, chives, cherry tomatoes, corn, cooked quinoa, lettuce wedges, and a dash of salt. Until you are ready to consume, cover with a lid and keep, preferably in a cool location.

Lentil Tabbouleh

Servings : 2

19 grams Protein

70 grams Carb

12 grams Fat

460 Cal Per Serving

Est. Prep Time: 10 mins

Est. Cook Time: 10 mins

Est. Total Time: 20 mins

Ingredients

- 100 g lentils (or 1 cup cooked lentils eg. tinned)
- 470 g vegetable broth (divided)
- 90 g couscous
- 1.5 tbsp olive oil
- 1 green onion (finely chopped)
- 1 clove garlic (minced)
- 2 sprigs mint, fresh (chopped)
- 3 sprigs parsley, fresh (chopped)
- 1 tbsp water

- 1 tbsp lemon juice (or 1 tsp white vinegar)
- Salt to taste
- 1 tomato (diced)
- ½ medium cucumber (diced)
- Salt and pepper to taste

Instructions

- lentils). Add the lentils and 1 1/2 cups of vegetable broth to a small pot. When the liquid reaches a rolling boil, cover the pan, reduce the heat, and cook the lentils until tender.
- Add the couscous to a bowl in the interim. Just enough hot vegetable broth should be added to cover the couscous, around 12 cup. Observe for ten minutes.
- Add onion, garlic, mint, parsley, water, lemon juice, salt, and olive oil to a small bowl. Combine and let sit until required.

- Cucumber and tomato are diced and added to the couscous.
- Add the cooked lentils and dressing afterward. Add salt and pepper to taste. To taste, add extra lemon. Done. Nice!

Best High-protein Tangy Tempeh Salad

Servings : 2

22 grams Protein

32 grams Carb

19 grams Fat

368 Cal Per Serving

Est. Prep Time: 5 mins

Est. Cook Time: 10 mins

Est. Total Time: 15 mins

Ingredients

- 6 radishes
- ½ cucumber
- 1 tsp salt
- 7 oz tempeh (7oz = 200g)
- 1 tbsp olive oil
- 1 cup green beans (or peas)
- 2 tbsp maple syrup
- 2 tbsp soy sauce
- 1 tbsp tomato paste (or ketchup)
- 1 tsp paprika

- ½ tsp sesame oil

Instructions

- Slice the cucumber and the radishes thinly after peeling them. Add a pinch of salt and place in a big bowl. After about ten minutes, you can tip away the extra water that the salt has drawn out.
- Cut the tempeh into small pieces while waiting.
- Chop the green beans roughly.
- After five minutes on medium heat, add the green beans, maple syrup, soy sauce, tomato paste, paprika, and sesame oil to the tempeh.
- After giving it a few more minutes to cook, combine it all in the bowl with the cucumber and radish. Mix it well, then dish it up and take a bite. Tempeh tastes best when consumed immediately.

Chickpea Spinach Salad

Servings : 2

23 grams Protein

56 grams Carb

32 grams Fat

579 Cal Per Serving

Est. Prep Time: 7 mins

Est. Cook Time: 7 mins

Est. Total Time: 14 mins

Ingredients

- 1 can chickpeas (drained and rinsed)(1 can = 435g)
- 1 handful spinach
- 3.5 oz low fat feta cheese (use regular if you prefer)(3.5oz = 100g)
- 1 small handful raisins
- 1 tbsp lemon juice (white or malt vinegar is also good)
- 3 tsp honey
- 3 tbsp olive oil

- ½ – 1 tsp cumin, ground
- 1 pinch salt
- ½ tsp chili flakes

Instructions

- Add the spinach, chickpeas, and cheese, chopped, to a large bowl.
- In a small bowl, combine the honey, oil, lemon juice, and raisins.
- Mix well after adding the cumin, salt, and pepper to the dressing basin.
- Dress the salad with a devilishly good dressing.
- Enjoy

Black Bean Lime Dip

Servings : 10

23 grams Protein

65 grams Carb

15 grams Fat

474 Cal Per Serving

Est. Prep Time: 5 mins

Est. Cook Time: 5 mins

Est. Total Time: 10 mins

Ingredients

- 1 cloves garlic
- 2.5 cm ginger, fresh (1 inch = 2.5 cm)
- 1 can black beans (1 can = 15.5 oz; 435g)
- 1 tbsp olive oil
- ½ lime (juiced) (maybe a little more)
- 10 tbsp water
- Salt and pepper to taste

Instructions

- Grate or finely chop the ginger and garlic. Then cook both for a few minutes in oil over medium heat in a big pot. Keep it from burning!
- Black beans should be rinsed and drained before being added to the pan.
- Add some water as you go, and continue to fry for a few more minutes.
- Finally, turn off the heat and stir in the lime juice, salt, and pepper.
- To create a smooth paste, mash everything together using a fork or potato masher.
- You may add it to salads, potatoes, toast, or just eat it plain as a high-protein snack.

Carrot and Red Lentil Soup

Servings : 2

28 grams Protein

79 grams Carb

12 grams Fat

534 Cal Per Serving

Est. Prep Time: 5 mins

Est. Cook Time: 20 mins

Est. Total Time: 25 mins

Ingredients

- 1 tbsp olive oil
- 2 carrot
- 1 onion
- 1250 ml vegetable broth
- 250 ml natural yogurt
- 200 g red lentils, dried

Instructions

- Grab a pot, turn the heat to low, and add the olive oil.
- Grate the garlic and cut the carrots and onion.
- Place them in the pot, let them cook for a couple of minutes, and then add the lentils.
- Stir a little to distribute the oil over the lentils (they open their pores which then tastes better).
- Yogurt and vegetable stock should be added.
- On low heat, let the soup simmer for 15 to 20 minutes.
- Add salt and pepper to taste.
- Including the lemon juice
- If you have access to one, puree it using a hand blender; if not, don't worry.

- Ready (eat with bread, add your preferred herbs for variety, and some extra yogurt or sour cream).

Lentil Salad

Servings : 2

22 grams Protein

73 grams Carb

19 grams Fat

529 Cal Per Serving

Est. Prep Time: 5 mins

Est. Cook Time: 7 mins

Est. Total Time: 12 mins

Ingredients

- 75 g cashews (½ cups = 75 g)
- 1 onion
- 1 tsp olive oil
- 1 chili / jalapeño
- 4 sun-dried tomatoes in oil
- 3 slices wholegrain bread (whole wheat)
- 235 g brown lentils, cooked (1 cup = 1/15oz / 235g lentils or a 400g can)
- 1 handful arugula/rocket (1 handful = 100 g)

- 2 tbsp balsamic vinegar
- Salt and pepper to taste
- 1 small handful raisins
- 1 tsp maple syrup

Instructions

- To enhance scent, roast the cashews in a skillet over a low heat for about three minutes. After that, place them in the salad dish.
- Slice the onion, then cook it in olive oil over low heat for about 3 minutes.
- Place the onion mixture in a large basin.
- The dried tomatoes and jalapenos should be chopped in the meantime. Cut the bread into large croutons. When the bread is crunchy, add them to the skillet and fry for an additional 2 minutes. It should work with the oil from the sun-dried tomatoes.

- Add salt and pepper to taste.
- Add the washed arugula to the bowl. Raisins are added.
- Include the lentils as well. Add salt, pepper, maple syrup, and balsamic vinegar for seasoning. Lastly, garnish with the croutons mixture. really tasty

Blueberry Banana Protein Smoothie

Servings : 1

27 grams Protein

71 grams Carb

14 grams Fat

506 Cal Per Serving

Est. Prep Time: 5 mins

Est. Cook Time: …mins

Est. Total Time: 10 mins

Ingredients

- 1 cup blueberries, frozen (fresh is fine too)
- 1 ripe banana (make sure they're soft and sweet! Keep some in the freezer like we do here)
- 1 cup milk of choice (we use soy milk)
- 1 tsp vanilla extract
- 4 oz low fat cottage cheese (use regular if you prefer*)
- 2 tbsp chia seeds

- 1 tsp lemon zest

Instructions

- Grate the lemon zest and combine it with the remaining ingredients in a blender.
- Then, blend.

Perfect Scrambled Eggs with Cheese

Servings : 2

22 grams Protein

21 grams Carb

13 grams Fat

327 Cal Per Serving

Est. Prep Time: 2 mins

Est. Cook Time: 3 mins

Est. Total Time: 5 mins

Ingredients

- 2 eggs
- 30 g cheddar cheese, grated (or Monterey Jack)
- ½ tsp olive oil (or butter)
- Salt and pepper to taste
- 1 slice whole grain bread

Instructions

- Put the butter or oil in a frying pan and heat it to medium.
- With a fork, quickly beat the eggs after breaking them into a bowl.
- Prepare the cheese by grating it.
- In the frying pan, pour the beaten eggs.
- The cheese is layered on top.
- Use a spatula to "pull" the eggs in from the side to the center as soon as they begin to almost immediately begin to harden.
- Pulling in should be repeated multiple times.
- The idea is that you'll have fresh, soft-boiled eggs; it doesn't take long. Really, it's difficult to undercook an egg, but it's simple to overcook one. You only need to heat the food for 2 to 3 minutes.
- You're finished when the egg has no more "watery" components. Remove from fire

immediately and place on plate, ideally on top of some delicious, hot, unbuttered bread.

- As desired, season with salt and pepper. Done!

Couscous Kaiserschmarrn

Servings : 2

22 grams Protein

50 grams Carb

10 grams Fat

376 Cal Per Serving

Est. Prep Time: 5 mins

Est. Cook Time: 15 mins

Est. Total Time: 20 mins

Ingredients

- 45 g couscous
- 85 ml milk of choice (eg. soy or oat milk)
- 2 large eggs
- 210 g Greek yogurt
- 1 tsp vanilla extract
- 1 tbsp sugar
- Pinch salt
- 30 g all purpose flour
- 1 tsp butter
- 80 g berries or fruit of choice

- Powdered sugar

Instructions

- Add the milk and couscous to a medium bowl.
- Add the Greek yogurt, sugar, salt, vanilla extract, and egg to a bowl. Mix until fully combined. When there are no lumps and the flour has been well mixed, add it next.
- Melt the butter in a pan. When it is very hot, add the kaiserschmarrn batter and cook it for 13–15 minutes over medium heat while covering the pan. Flip around halfway through or when the surface starts to dry.
- After being cooked, break the pieces into two dishes. Serve with extra Greek yogurt, berries, or other fruits of your choice, and top with powdered sugar.

Beans and Eggs

Servings : 2

24 grams Protein

39 grams Carb

17 grams Fat

406 Cal Per Serving

Est. Prep Time: 10 mins

Est. Cook Time: 5 mins

Est. Total Time: 15 mins

Ingredients

- ½ tbsp olive oil
- 1 clove garlic (smashed)
- 75 g cherry tomatoes (about 10-15 cherry tomatoes depending of the size)
- ½ tsp thyme, dried
- 1 tsp oregano, dried
- ½ tbsp red wine vinegar or balsamic vinegar
- 3 tbsp water
- ½ tsp honey

- 180 g white beans (cooked or canned)
- Salt and pepper to taste
- 4 eggs
- ¼ tsp cumin, ground
- ¼ tsp chili flakes
- 2 tsp olive oil
- 2 slices whole grain toast
- Salt and pepper to taste

Instructions

- Olive oil and a crushed garlic clove should be placed in a small pot over medium heat. Cook the garlic clove until it starts to turn brown.
- Add entire cherry tomatoes, thyme, oregano, salt, and black pepper. Mix and simmer tomatoes until some of them burst open and are tender.

- Add beans, honey, vinegar, and water. Once combined, heat the beans through. Keep back until required.
- In a medium-sized bowl, whisk the eggs until the white and yolk are completely blended. Salt, black pepper, chili flakes, and cumin should all be combined.
- Over low heat, add olive oil to an 8" nonstick pan. When a thin layer of cooked egg emerges around the edge of the skillet, add the eggs and cook them, stirring occasionally.
- Eggs should be pushed across the bottom of the skillet and all the way around it using a rubber spatula and broad sweeping motions. For about 2 minutes, keep moving the eggs around and across the skillet; they should still appear runny on top.

- Divide immediately between 2 plates, season with sea salt and additional black pepper, and serve with beans and whole-wheat toast.

10-Minute Vegan Tempeh Sandwich

Servings : 2

21 grams Protein

51 grams Carb

32 grams Fat

547 Cal Per Serving

Est. Prep Time: 3 mins

Est. Cook Time: 7 mins

Est. Total Time: 10 mins

Ingredients

- 4 slices wholegrain bread
- 80 grams tempeh (in 8 slices)
- 2 rocket (arugula)
- 100 g sun-dried tomatoes in oil
- 1 tbsp olive oil
- 2 tbsp vinegar (balsamic, malt or wine vinegar)
- 2 tbsp soy sauce
- 2 tsp maple syrup
- 1 avocado

- ½ lemon (juiced)
- Salt and pepper to taste

Instructions

- Oil-fry the tempeh after slicing it. Add the soy sauce, vinegar, and maple syrup after a few minutes. For a another 3–4 minutes, stir and cook.
- Chop the dried tomatoes while waiting.
- Remove the avocado's flesh with a spoon, and place it in a bowl with the lemon juice, salt, and pepper. Mix everything together.
- ½ lemon, pepper and salt as desired
- Over half the slices of bread, spread the avocado.
- Lay the bread slices with the rinsed rocket on top. The diced dried tomatoes should be added.

- Place the tempeh on the slices of bread with the rocket after it is done.
- flatbread with avocado on top of it. Done!

Fresh & Minty Pineapple and Spinach Smoothie

Servings : 1

24 grams Protein

58 grams Carb

14 grams Fat

438 Cal Per Serving

Est. Prep Time: 7 mins

Est. Cook Time: 7 mins

Est. Total Time: 14 mins

Ingredients

- 115 g pineapple chunks (preferably frozen)
- 1 small sprig mint, fresh
- 140 g Greek yogurt
- ¼ tsp vanilla extract
- 40 g baby spinach
- 1 tbsp flax seeds
- 1 tbsp cashews
- 1.5 tsp maple syrup

- 2 tbps rolled oats
- 1 ice cubes

Instructions

- Blender with all components added.
- Blend until smooth and well combined. The solids' textures shouldn't be seen, and everything should be as smooth as possible.
- If you want a stronger mint flavor, taste and add more mint leaves.

Bread Pudding

Servings : 2

21 grams Protein

50 grams Carb

13 grams Fat

405 Cal Per Serving

Est. Prep Time: 15 mins

Est. Cook Time: 15 mins

Est. Total Time: 30 mins

Ingredients

- 2 eggs
- 180 ml milk of choice (we like soy or oat milk)
- 1 ¾ tbsp sugar
- 1 tsp vanilla extract
- ½ tsp cinnamon
- 130 g wholegrain bread (old, but you can use fresh too)
- 4 tbsp blueberries/raspberries
- 2 tbsp almonds (sliced)

- 4 tbsp Greek yogurt (for serving)

Instructions

- Set your oven to 250 C.
- Add the eggs, milk, sugar, vanilla essence, and ground cinnamon to a medium bowl. Completely combine by blending.
- Bread that has been torn into pieces approximately an inch long, blueberries, raspberries, seeds, or almonds can all be added. Mix until you can see that every piece of bread is in contact with the liquid.
- A tiny baking mold should be lightly coated with oil or brushed with oil. Spread the bread pudding mixture evenly on the surface.
- Bake on the center oven rack for 10 minutes. Then move the bread pudding

to the topmost rack, preheat the grill or broiler to its maximum setting, and bake for 3 to 5 minutes, or until the top is golden brown.

- Serving bread pudding with a dollop of greek yoghurt

Spinach and Chickpea Bake

Servings : 2

23 grams Protein

23 grams Carb

17 grams Fat

330 Cal Per Serving

Est. Prep Time: 15 mins

Est. Cook Time: 20 mins

Est. Total Time: 35 mins

Ingredients

- 115 g spinach
- 30 g parsley, fresh
- 12 g basil, fresh
- 120 ml water
- 1 tsp olive oil
- ½ red onion (diced)
- 1 garlic (minced)
- 220 g chickpeas (canned or cooked)
- 1 ½ tsp lemon juice
- ¼ tsp cumin, ground

- ¼ tsp nutmeg
- ¼ tsp paprika
- 4 eggs
- 60 g ricotta cheese (crumbled)
- Salt and pepper to taste
- Paprika (garnish)
- Jalapeño (sliced, garnish)
- Basil, fresh (garnish)
- Parsley, fresh (garnish)

Instructions

- Blanching the spinach's leaves is only necessary if it is fresh and not frozen. A small pot of salted, boiled water and a dish of ice water should be ready. Boiling water should be added to the spinach, parsley, and basil. Blanch for 15 to 20 seconds. As soon as the leaves have begun to cool fully, sift them and put them in ice water. Press the leaves against the sieve to release all the absorbed water to separate the water from the leaves.

- Blend water and green leaves until they are processed and smooth.
- set the oven to 400 degrees.
- The olive oil should be heated over medium-low heat in a medium cast iron pan or oven-safe pan. Add the minced garlic and onion. Cook until the edges start to become golden.
- Add chickpeas, spinach green juice, lemon juice, cumin, paprika, nutmeg, and salt and pepper to taste after turning off the heat. Assemble by combining.
- Crack an egg into each of the four little wells you just made using a spoon. Add paprika, black pepper, and salt to taste. About 10 minutes into baking, the eggs should be just set.

- To serve, sprinkle green leaves, chili flakes, and crumbled ricotta on top.

German Bauernfrühstuck

Servings : 1

25 grams Protein

62 grams Carb

22 grams Fat

540 Cal Per Serving

Est. Prep Time: 5 mins

Est. Cook Time: 25 mins

Est. Total Time: 30 mins

Ingredients

- 300 g potato (2 medium potatoes = 150g each)
- 2 tsp olive oil
- 1 small onion
- 2 eggs
- 6 g rosemary, fresh (¼ cup fresh = 1 tbsp dried)
- 6 g basil, fresh (¼ cup fresh = 1 tbsp dried)
- Salt and pepper to taste

- 60 g low fat mozzarella
- 1 tbsp vinegar

Instructions

- Slice the potatoes into small pieces. slicing the onion
- For 20 minutes, cook the sliced potatoes in olive oil in a large frying pan over medium heat. Add the diced onion halfway. Use a lid to cook them a little bit more quickly. It won't crisp up if you stir it too frequently.
- Give the eggs a quick whisk with a fork after breaking them into a cup. Add
- Add the salt, pepper, mozzarella, herbs, and eggs.
- Cook the egg for an additional 2 minutes or until it is done.
- Pour a little vinegar in.
- Done!

Creamy Cashew Milkshake

Servings : 1

17.2 grams Protein

61.6 grams Carb

19.4 grams Fat

431 Cal Per Serving

Est. Prep Time: 5 mins

Est. Cook Time: 5 mins

Est. Total Time: 10 mins

Ingredients

- 250 ml soy milk (other milk is fine as well – use gluten-free if needed) (1 cup = 250ml)
- 1 medium, ripe banana
- 3 tsp cacao powder (real cacao, not the nesquik type of stuff)
- 3 tbsp cashews
- 1 pinch salt

Instructions

- Blend the cashews until they are nicely smooth for about three minutes after adding the milk, banana, powder, and salt to the blender.
- Put in the refrigerator to chill, or drink right away! Simple, done!

High Protein Yogurt Breakfast with Raspberry Compote

Servings : 1

22 grams Protein

32 grams Carb

13 grams Fat

324 Cal Per Serving

Est. Prep Time: 8 mins

Est. Cook Time: 10 mins

Est. Total Time: 18 mins

Ingredients

- 170 g raspberries
- 2 tbsp sugar
- ⅛ tsp baking soda (optional)
- ¼ cup water
- 1 tsp orange zest (plus more for serving (optional))
- 1 tsp vanilla extract
- 350 g Greek yogurt
- 3 tbsp pistachios (chopped)

- 2 tbsp chia seeds

Instructions

- The raspberries, water, sugar, chia seeds, baking soda, orange zest (if used), and vanilla should all be combined in a small pot. Cook the raspberries at medium-low heat until the little bits are soft and crumbling apart, the liquid has released and started to thicken, and you have a syrupy compote (about 10 minutes). Let it cool.
- Yogurt should be served in two bowls. Add some orange zest, pistachios that have been chopped, and the compote on top.

Smoked Tofu Breakfast Egg

Servings : 3

22 grams Protein

11 grams Carb

19 grams Fat

298 Cal Per Serving

Est. Prep Time: 10 mins

Est. Cook Time: 20 mins

Est. Total Time: 30 mins

Ingredients

- 6 eggs
- 1 leek
- 2 small onion
- 160 g smoked tofu (6oz = 160g)
- 60 g cheddar cheese, grated
- ½ tsp salt
- 1 tsp olive oil

Instructions

- Set the oven to 200 °C or 390 °F.
- Tofu should be cut into little squares. Slice the onion and chop the leek.
- Tofu, leek, onion, grated cheese, eggs, and salt are all combined in a mixing bowl.
- Spread some olive oil inside the muffin tins. Fill each muffin slot evenly with the mixture.
- 1 teaspoon olive oil
- 200°C/390°F for 20 minutes of baking
- The prepared egg muffins for breakfast

Volume Conversions

Cup	Ounce	Milliliter	TableSpoon
8 Cup	64 oz	1895 ml	128
6 Cup	48 oz	1420 ml	96
5 Cup	40 oz	1180 ml	80
4 Cup	32 oz	960 ml	64
2 Cup	16 oz	480 ml	32
1 Cup	8 oz	240 ml	16
¾ Cup	6 oz	177 ml	12
⅔ Cup	5 oz	158 ml	11
½ Cup	4 oz	118ml	8
⅜ Cup	3 oz	90 ml	6
⅓ Cup	2.5 oz	79 ml	5.5

¼ Cup	2 oz	59 ml	4
⅛ Cup	1 oz	30 ml	3
1/16 Cup	½ oz	15 ml	1

Fahrenheit	Celsius
100	37
150	65
200	93
250	121
300	150
325	160
350	180
375	190
400	200
435	220
450	230
500	260
525	274
550	288

Weight Conversion

Imperial	Metric
1/2oz	15g
1oz	29g
2oz	57g
3oz	85g
4oz	113g
5oz	141g
6oz	170g
8oz	227g
10oz	283g
12oz	340g
13oz	369g

14oz	397g
15oz	425g
1lb	453g

1 tablespoon = 3 teaspoons = 15 milliliters

4 tablespoons = 1/4 cup = 60 milliliters

1 ounce = 2 tablespoons = 30 milliliters

1 cup = 8 oz. = 250 milliliters

1 pint = 2 cups = 500 milliliters

1 quart = 4 cups = 950 milliliters

1 quart = 2 pints = 950 milliliters

1 gallon = 4 quarts = 3800 milliliters = 3.8 liters

Printed in Great Britain
by Amazon

47701268R00109